LEAP TO TRACK

Catherine S. Vodrey

2009

East Liverpool, Ohio
www.WordBanquet.com

Copyright © 2009
by Catherine S. Vodrey
ALL RIGHTS RESERVED.

ISBN #978-0-578-02269-7

Visit the author's web site at
www.WordBanquet.com

> . . . standing absolutely motionless,
> at a slight angle to the universe.
>
> E. M. FORSTER

> I do not feel like spending
> the rest of my life writing books
> that no one will read. It is not
> as though I wanted to write them.
>
> SAMUEL BECKETT

*This is dedicated
to Gavin, of course—
patience, kindness.*

Heartfelt gratitude to my true-blues:

Henry and Lillian Klein
Sarah Vodrey
Allison Corbett
Katie Hoffman
Gary Middleton
Bridgette Collins
Michael Klein
Tracy Mangano
Helen Gricks
Sally Cappelli
Mitch Osborne
Trish Disch
Lee Bares
Zylphia Ford
Bill and Amy Belden

Many thanks
to my friend Bill Crawford (again)
who came through when I needed his
incomparable technical expertise (again).

The author is grateful to . . .

Lawrence K. Altman; Anne Barnard; Graham Bowley; John Branch; John M. Broder; Cara Buckley; Elisabeth Bumiller; Marian Burros; Noam Cohen; Anahad Cooper; Sam Dagher; Shaila Dewan; Rachel Donadio; Joe Drape; Steve Erlanger; Manny Fernandez; Steve Freiss; Jeffrey Gettleman; Peter S. Goodman; Penelope Green; Anemona Hartocollis; William Harwood; Javier C. Hernandez; Carl Hulse; Nicholas Kulish; Marc Lacey; Ron Lieber; Adam Liptak; Robert Mackey; Juliet Macur; Mark Mazzetti; Stephen Mihm; Solomon Moore; Errol Morris; Seth Mydans; Nicole Neroulias; Anahad O'Connor; Sharon Otterman; Dennis Overbye; Tara Parker-Pope; Ronald Pies, MD; Elisabetta Povoledo; Campbell Robertson; Larry Rohter; John Schwartz; Alan Schwarz; Katharine Q. Seelye; Sabrina Tavernise; Ginger Thompson; Ian Urbina; Joyce Wadler; Bruce Weber; Michael Wilson; Robert F. Worth; Jim Yardley; Jeff Zeleny; and Katie Zezima.

A NOTE ON THE POEMS

In 2008 and 2009, searching for something to get me in the habit of writing every day, I turned to newspaper headlines. The poem titles herein consist of headlines from a single national newspaper's web site.

Generally, I stuck to headlines from the front page but occasionally, I looked within the paper's sections. The dates on which the headlines appeared are listed immediately below each title. The poems appear in chronological order.

I was asked to use neither the newspaper's nor the reporters' names.

TABLE OF CONTENTS

OBAMA SPEAKS TO GERMANY . . . 1
CHINA'S LEADERS 2
GEORGIA AND RUSSIA 3
EDWARDS ADMITS TO AFFAIR . . . 4
IN THE STANDS 5
CHINESE GRAB GOLD 7
A BLIND BOXER 9
DR. DOOM 11
WHO KNEW WHAT WHEN? 12
SURVIVORS IN GEORGIA 13
WHAT GEORGE ORWELL 15
NEWCOMERS ADJUST 17
STORM STRIKES LAND 19
SEVEN YEARS LATER 21
REDEFINING DEPRESSION 22
BUT WILL IT WORK? 24
STATUS OF DEBATE 25
'IS MY MONEY SAFE?' 26
WRECKAGE OF FOSSETT'S 27
THE HEARTBEAT JOB 29
MOUNTAIN CLIMBING 30
SORRY, I CAN'T FIND 31
EVEN KEEL FOR OBAMA 32
FOR McCAIN, LIGHTER END 34
AFTER U.S. BREAKTHROUGH . . . 35
FIREFIGHTERS GAIN A HOLD . . . 37
FAILING HOME ECONOMICS 39

LACK OF PREPAREDNESS	40
FIRST U. S. FACE TRANSPLANT	41
BREAD OF LIFE	43
OBAMA IS SWORN IN	44
ARREST SAID TO BE NEAR	45
IN A HISTORICAL HOUSE	46
PORTRAIT OF SHAKESPEARE	48
FORMER SLA MEMBER	50
LEAP TO TRACK	52
NATASHA RICHARDSON	54
WHITE HOUSE	56
TRAVELERS, YOUR TOUR BUS	58
SON OF SYLVIA PLATH	60
AS CLINTON VISITS MEXICO	63
RUSSIAN ROCKET	65
SWEPT UP	66
WHOSE FATHER WAS HE?	67
APOLOGY OFFERED	69
AMID BINGHAMTON GUNFIRE	71
DEATH TOLL	73
ANSWERING BASEBALL'S	74
A MOMENT OF HEROISM	76
ROMEO IS LATE FOR DINNER	78
CAPTAIN STILL HELD	80
SITE OF '07 MASS SHOOTING	81
A MEXICAN TRADITION	82
GAY VOWS	84

LAST VOYAGE 85
DERBY FAVORITES 87
18 YEARS IN THE MAKING 88

OBAMA SPEAKS TO GERMANY ON EUROPEAN TIES
Friday, July 25th, 2008

I'm not a tie man, myself.
I come across as a guy
Who wouldn't wear a tie
If he could help it.

But I want the job, and I know
There will be ties involved.
Here a tie, there a tie,
Everywhere a tie, Thai.

So I'm speaking to you on European ties.
You know what I'm saying here:
I'm for them, European and otherwise.
Ich bin Obama.

In closing, on European ties,
My stance is this:
They're good.
A big pile of them, soft underfoot,
A little unbalancing now that
I'm standing
Here, a little bit slippery,
This slope.

CHINA'S LEADERS TRY TO IMPRESS AND REASSURE WORLD
Friday, August 8th, 2008

We are happy to host the world
At the Olympics,
Which is only a gathering of athletes
And no place for politics.
Welcome, Mr. President.

Protests have no place here.
We accept differences of opinion
And encourage open dialogue
In the marked areas.

Watch as we release our own invention
Convincing night
It is day: fireworks
State that they are a constellation
Blossoming over the universe
Of Beijing.

We are whole
And complete unto ourselves.
We need no one else.

Watch, please.

GEORGIA AND RUSSIA NEARING ALL-OUT WAR
Saturday, August 9th, 2008

We are a land of peanut farmers
Who like to mind our own business
Like all right-thinking people should. So
We don't know why
The Russians are mad at us.

Maybe we said something
About their women
Or their alcohol consumption;
We don't remember.

We don't think we said anything,
But translation's a bitch.

EDWARDS ADMITS TO AFFAIR IN 2006
Saturday, August 9th, 2008

I started to believe that I was special
And became increasingly egocentric
And narcissistic.
And dumb;
My wife would tell you I should admit
To dumb as well.
I'm not as smart as I look.

I followed this well-worn path,
But really, I didn't even see it until
I was on it.
And if at the end of the path stood
An attractive woman who wanted
Nothing more than to look at me and
Listen to me, well, I didn't know
This was the way it was done.
I didn't see it.
I was naïve. My mistake.

Sure, I'll take a test.
Any test you want.
My Lord and my wife have forgiven me.
Tests are easy.

IN THE STANDS, UNEXPECTED VOIDS
Tuesday, August 12th, 2008

I feel the world at my back.
My concentration on the task
At hand
Doesn't preclude knowing
That all the world is watching.

They say the television ratings are good.
People are watching.
Tickets are hard to come by.
Yet there are empty seats
For my event,
Which is not swimming
Or gymnastics
Or basketball.

But: there are tens
Of thousands of people
At home, in classrooms, in the bar
I never have the nerve
Or the time to walk into
At home.

I am known to more people
Than I will meet in my entire life.

And from their branched locations,
All arrowing out from mine,
They all pay attention as
I rise, I move.

I am thunderously decisive.
Gold shows the same
Bright smile to everyone.

CHINESE GRAB GOLD IN GYMNASTICS
Wednesday, August 13th, 2008

There is talk
That we are not our age.

There is talk
That we are missing teeth,
Inches,
Pounds.

There is no way,
Some feel,
That we can be sixteen.

Let us distract you
From the numbers.
Watch as we dance
A knife's-edge beam.
We inscribe the air
With brief calligraphy,
Which, by the way, we invented.

Watch as we zig-zag
On uneven bars—
Only two lines! Nothing to it.
We orbit the bars:

An age compressed
To an instant.
Our planetary tour
Of the fixed points is
A radiant whirl
Of red movement.

On the mat, we stand,
Each a *Jin Ren*
Overseeing the blue world
Laid at our feet. We stride,
Stamp, launch, revolt
Against gravity,
A second's victory as head
Spins past feet,
Hips, arms, everything:

We are points on a graph,
We fit the corner
By making a right angle with our feet,
We look up, we look down,
We are girls, we are all
Levers and gears.

A BLIND BOXER INSPIRES UGANDA
Friday, August 15th, 2008

My doctor said there was nothing
He could do.

I sat in the dark, always;
Day or night were all the same to me.
I sat
For months
And thought about it.
Then
I decided to get up.

I run each morning, a boy
At my wrist to guide me.
The ground is cruel and tricky.
I get no warning
Before a fall, though the boy
Tries his best.
We both do. He takes me

Back to the gym and I fight
Anyone blinded by cloth.

I train and train.

I dent the bag; each punch
Throws off dust I can't see.

I breathe it in and it goes
To where it's always dark,
Inside me.

DR. DOOM
Friday, August 15th, 2008

He is inked in cobalt
And black, shadow colors
Which limn the ghastly
Planes of his face.

Corners and doors
Are what
He peers around,
Always hidden
By choice. He likes to plant
Doubt and fear, likes to watch
Them take hold.
Vining question marks
Casting tendrils
In reverse: away
From light,
Towards dark.

WHO KNEW WHAT WHEN?
Monday, August 18th, 2008

Who knew what when?

Well, how long do you have?

Kennedy knew he'd order the cigars
Before signing the embargo.

Joan of Arc must have had an inkling
That claiming conversations with God
Would end in her pyre.

Newton, Carver, Curie,
Einstein, Darwin:
Too much to go into here. Essentially,
They knew everything long before
Anyone else even thought to consider it.

Imagine, having these universal keys
In your head
And being unable to tell anyone
When it first dawned
For fear they'd use a different key
On a door between the two of you.

SURVIVORS IN GEORGIA
TELL OF ETHNIC KILLINGS
Tuesday, August 19th, 2008

It is the same veil which covered
Phnom Penh
And Krakow
And Darfur.

Every kernel has a silk;
Every one of the dozens,
Hundreds or thousands
Grew out of something.
The numbers are past
Any fringe of understanding.
But even just one has
Somewhere a past,
A mother or wife or daughter
Waiting: eyes closed.

Some of them are shivering,
Teeth chattering in fear as they face
A wall
Where the sun mercilessly
Illustrates in compatriot shadow
Every pock, every divot.
Boys, some of them:
There is no birthday count

By these powers.

Some are still on
Their morning cup of coffee,
Heads bent to steam,
Not seeing
The aphotic approach.

WHAT GEORGE ORWELL WROTE, 70 YEARS LATER TO THE DAY
Sunday, August 24th, 2008

It is before we have become involved,
But I know we will.

Neville Chamberlain lays his words
On the floor and gives them a push
With his fingernail.

Out from under the door they come
As he peeks through the mail slot.
He hopes they will
Inform and calm.
Instead, they precede the fall
Of the Netherlands, Belgium and France.
He stands behind number ten,
But risks the thousands.

How to be calm
As our companion countries
Slacken and lie in the mud?

I look out the window
And watch the blackberries ripen.
I can see it from hour to hour,

Blood to black,
Until they are ready
To pick.

NEWCOMERS ADJUST, EVENTUALLY, TO NEW YORK
Tuesday, August 26th, 2008

The first thing is the crowd:
You can't believe it.
Everywhere you go:

Shoulders rubbing against yours
And someone offended by it
And cursing—you!
Cursing you.
You can't believe it.

Next are the buildings;
You feel like an ant at the base
Of a fence.
You can't believe it.
You're never going to find
This place.

The smells: some of them
Are good, but most
Are urine, garbage
And something stale you can't
Identify.

So when you get used to all of it,
In fact, expect it,
In fact, start to
Believe it,
You're there.

STORM STRIKES LAND WEST OF NEW ORLEANS
Monday, September 1st, 2008

All of us in the weather center
Have been watching and waiting.
Everyone looks to us,
While we look up to sky on screens
And down to graphs.
Our nursery game:
Show and tell.

Satellites show us
What brew
God is concocting,
Where it will be spilled
And whether the mix
Will consume
The coast.

It's a card trick:
We can watch
All we want
Without understanding the sleight.

When we see that it isn't
A sledgehammer like Katrina,

We all sit back a little.

Breathe and calm.

We see just the black hem
Instead of the whole shroud
Dropped to cover.

SEVEN YEARS LATER, 9/11 SURVIVORS SEARCH FOR NORMALCY
Tuesday, September 9th, 2008

The eleven is what my life looks like:
One life before and
One after.

After months of forced sleep,
I awoke to see my weeping husband
At the foot of a strange metal bed.

It took me a moment to realize:
I was in the bed.

He bowed his head
When I said his name.

I didn't think to ask for a mirror
Until the second day.

REDEFINING DEPRESSION AS MERE SADNESS
Monday, September 15th, 2008

Thomas à Kempis wrote
That we all have proper sorrows
Of the soul.
What is proper about sorrow?

What is tidy and easily defined about the
Loose, bleeding edge of sadness?

Perhaps the sting of tears
At the dart well-planted;
The disappointment of the
Lost opportunity;
The mortification of the blind date.
Walking home and thinking,
I will never go on another blind date,
Which maybe means
I will never go on
Another date.

Which means that you will walk
Up these steps,
Up to your apartment
Empty of other people,
Up to your bowl situated

Alone in the sink,
Its spoon an oar cast in the white sea.

You will sit in the night living room,
Your feet meeting a stalk of light
From the street
And no one will say,
Why are you sitting in the dark?

BUT WILL IT WORK?
Saturday, September 20th, 2008

Money and rumor
Are in the same black
Domino array.
Like some island language,
Each clicks the next to submit.

The domino at the end
Still stands,
Stands still,
Despite the inertial freight
Approaching in sure stages.

Each tiny advance,
Each shuttering of the light
Between each dark slice
Weights the storm
Until the storm
Becomes the story
And no one remembers
Each microscopic wink.

STATUS OF DEBATE
REMAINS UNCERTAIN
Thursday, September 25th, 2008

One calls for delay;
The other for debate.

The economy whirls its green tornado
Around the decision.
Everything, everything
Is urgent.

Behind the podiums,
The rippling flag with its blood,
Purity, liberty, valor.

Two spots, each marked:
Will one remain empty,
Its resident denying his face
To the cameras?

'IS MY MONEY SAFE?' AND OTHER QUESTIONS TO ASK
Monday, September 29th, 2008

Is my money safe?
Did he really mean to say that?
Do we have to invite them?
How much will it cost?
When will it be ready?
What's the deal with this rash?
Does that include tax?
Does it come with instructions?

WRECKAGE OF FOSSETT'S PLANE IS FOUND
Tuesday, October 2nd, 2008

I know what I'm doing.
I'm off the trail,
But I know the way.

Not even birds pierce the air;
Only the sound of my own footfalls
Brackets where I am.

A magma of light pours
Over my back. A square of it returns
To me, up from the ground,
Shining back the sun's name.
When I pick it up,
I realize it's
An ID with the name *Steve Fossett* on it.
All around it are hundred-dollar bills,
Stiff from rainfall
And neglect.

I gather everything up.
I take it home,
Show my wife.

She tells me who he is
And how long he's been missing.

I think of his wife
In the void for a full year,
Waiting, waiting
As I bring her
The day she never wanted.

THE HEARTBEAT JOB
Saturday, October 4th, 2008

A bucket passed from one man
To the next and now
Possibly to a woman.

As though for a fire;
As though one bucket could
Put anything out.

MOUNTAIN CLIMBING
BAD FOR THE BRAIN
Monday, October 20th, 2008

Well, sure,
If you land on your head.

SORRY, I CAN'T FIND YOUR NAME
Wednesday, October 22nd, 2008

Brave new world!
In which thousands of voters
Can be dropped into the rabbit hole,
Voiceless of protest.
This blazing work
Achieved with a single keystroke
By a single official.
(Official what?)

Shouldn't it be harder
To dissolve an entire town?

The official goes to work.
He sits at his computer
And uses the keyboard
As a diving platform
From which to launch 8,000 names.
One by one in rapid succession,
Sparks from a fire, they vanish
Into the fabric
Of the air.

He glances out his window
At the parking lot, he
Thinks about coffee.

EVEN KEEL FOR OBAMA IN FINAL TURN TO ELECTION
Sunday, November 2nd, 2008

He has said everything
Thousands of times.

He must say everything
Again
Only a few more times, for a few
More days, and then
He can be silent
In the booth as he checks
His own name.

Depending on how it goes, he may
Say everything
To the world that night.

He is a scrimshaw
Framed in a plane window,
A lightning rod on a stage,
A third of the embrace
He shares with his daughters.

His grandmother is dying
On an island,

Palm fronds fringing the picture
In his mind.

He travels to her
One last time, travels
From her,
Bears in mind
That she was his starting point,
The runner's blocks,
Some of the soil
From which he grew.

FOR McCAIN, LIGHTER END
AFTER YEARS ON THE TRAIL
Sunday, November 2nd, 2008

We are all his friends,
He says.

My friends, my friends,
Says this man alone in a crowd.

He beseeches us.
He has been to hell and back
And is willing to talk.

He is upstanding: a hero,
A father, a husband,
A senator, a son and grandson,
A military man who knows
What it is to be tested.
He is
Everything that is wrong
And right
With the dream we dare to name
American.

AFTER U.S. BREAKTHROUGH, EUROPE LOOKS IN MIRROR
Tuesday, November 11th, 2008

We predate
Mirrors.

We began when only a lake
Could show us our rippled selves,
Any passing breeze
Dashing our faces into mosaic.

Viking marauders, French troops,
German tribes: every permutation
Of white you can imagine.
Spilled blood, seed and money
Across the plains and mountains.
Descent
To now presents itself
Vividly in that red hair,
That Gallic nose or Teutonic
Reserve. Still,

The mix grows darker with migration
And the migration unsettles.

We look at America

As a mirror now, we look
To America for reflection, but
We do not yet see ourselves yet;
We are
Too far away.

FIREFIGHTERS GAIN A HOLD IN CALIFORNIA
Monday, November 17th, 2008

Everything is tinder out here;
Everything presents itself as food
To a hunger like this.

Most of the fires are big these days,
Swallowing down houses,
Trees, cars. Nothing is an obstacle
Before a thing that requires only air
To live and move.

The heat of it
Makes everything an oasis,
Shimmering like an oiled lens
We look through.

We cast water into the brightness,
We dig trenches, we warn
Families from their homes.

Some of them leave, some
Stay and try, but they don't speak
The language we do, and are helpless

Before this livid thief,
About to steal everything
They own.

FAILING HOME ECONOMICS
Wednesday, November 19th, 2008

There is a rustle at the base
Of every spine, a knowing
That disaster may be closer
Than we'd thought.

In fact, we never thought.
We bought.
We bought and charged and drank wine
We had no business drinking.
We added on, we shot our wad,
We rationalized, we begged,
Borrowed and stole.

And now this:
Really looking,
Really seeing
What's what
And the signs on everything
Saying
What everything costs.

LACK OF PREPAREDNESS COMES BRUTALLY TO LIGHT
Wednesday, December 3rd, 2008

I would have told you
We had everything, starting
With our passports.

Our faces, our accents, our homelands
Betrayed us.

We are taken because of who we are,
Though we are no one
To these young men.

How can they
Do any of this?
How can they haul us down the stairs,
Into the lobby and
Make us lie down on the floor?

We hear sirens.
The marble tiles are cool
Against our cheeks.
There is a hellish
Bouquet of bullets and fire
Overhead.

FIRST U. S. FACE
TRANSPLANT DESCRIBED
Wednesday, December 17th, 2008

No one who knows me
Knows the face I wear now.

The doctors pushed me under the surface
As though underwater
And as though rising to the surface
With a sheen of wet on my skin,
I came out of it
With a new landscape
Over my skull.

The eyelids are mine
From before.
The forehead, the temples.
These are not defining features.

Those that are now mine
Were hers, a woman laid out
As though on a banquet table
That's been picked over.

They took what they needed
From her, what I needed

From her, and they draped it
Like muslin over a chair.

They stitched it to me,
To the curves and shadows and
Tucked-away places where the scars
Might show less.

I am me underneath
What you would recognize
As her.

BREAD OF LIFE, BAKED IN RHODE ISLAND
Wednesday, December 24th, 2008

The sacred tumbles out
Of a stainless steel drum
Onto the blue conveyor belt, where it
Joins thousands of other shards
Of flour and water:
The body of Christ.

Maybe if you look at it
As though each piece were a molecule
Or an atom, the tiniest
Of parts of a whole,
You can make the leap
To faith.

Or maybe it doesn't need to be
That concrete. Maybe just saying,
We do not presume to come to this,
Thy table
Accepts the inexplicable.
We presume nothing.
We accept.

OBAMA IS SWORN IN AS THE 44th PRESIDENT
Tuesday, January 20th, 2009

It could be the universe,
A field of stars or another
Kind of field:
Wheat or corn, anything tall
And waving with the icy breeze.

So many people, all planted
In place, all turned in one direction
To see what is very new this day.

They face him as he faces the sun,
Lays his hand
On the book and recites
The constant vows.

**ARREST SAID
TO BE NEAR IN
CHANDRA LEVY'S MURDER**
Saturday, February 21st, 2009

How does anyone disappear?
But our daughter did.

She left her apartment and
Turned to vanish.
Her steps led her
Into a noxious fame: the same
Photograph over and over.
On paper,
She stopped aging forever.

We dropped a stone
Into a well and never
Heard it land. But
We still listen.

A year later, someone
Found something,
Some part of her that they call
Remains. It's all that remains.
A shoe, a lace,
A jacket. Bones.
How can we imagine bones?

IN A HISTORICAL HOUSE, AN AUCTION OF LINCOLN MEMORABILIA
Friday, February 27th, 2009

Three bronze oil lamps lit their wedding:
Burnished her gown, twinned
Themselves in the mirror, turned to gold
In rings and earbobs.

They are not much of themselves,
But for the nearness
Of the couple they lit,
They are invaluable.

The buyer imagines,
If he can,
That he is in that room,
Lit by those lamps, witnessing
This monumental man
And this diminutive woman
Agreeing to love and to honor.

Here in the future,
The buyer imagines that he could
Say something, could tell them what,
Like every bridal couple,
They don't know.

They know
Nothing of what lies
In their particular path:
Many sons—theirs,
A nation's.
A war, a theatre,
And a final handsome stranger
With a hard and glossy darkness
In his hand.

All of this is known
As completely to the buyer
As it is unknown to them,
These pre-legendary innocents
Who clasp newlywed hands
In the lamplight.

PORTRAIT OF SHAKESPEARE UNVEILED, 399 YEARS LATE
Monday, March 9th, 2009

He looks beyond:
Alert, staring into the middle distance,
Attentive as the populations stored
In his head
Conduct their many businesses.

Lovers are dying, fools are jesting,
Men are howling at the storm,
Or fate,
Or their fathers.
No matter what their circumstance,
All speak a glittering truth.
So keen is his understanding
That even denials made by any of them
Portray a true face constructed,
Lifelike, of words.

Some are fully his; some are historic.
Though all now
Strut only in his mind's eye,
They are so real as to be ourselves. They
Feel everything, they
Are engaged in every life event, they

Are all the world.
And all the world's a stage for him,
A stage which we
Watch as he sets his creations
Not in a garden, but in a globe.

We witness
Them fight the ancient fights,
Succumb to antique temptations
And get what they each want,
Or not,
In the way we all do.

FORMER SYMBIONESE LIBERATION ARMY MEMBER RELEASED FROM PRISON
Tuesday, March 17th, 2009

I was Kathleen;
I am Sara Jane.

Born and made, I took my
American life and made it my
American life. Some would say it was
Upside-down, backwards, or some other
Form of *not right*.

I was at that bank in 1975,
But it wasn't my gun.
I wasn't even sure
Why money was the object
That day, or how that woman ended
Up slumping against the counter,
A new red rose pinned to her blouse
Where nothing had bloomed before.

It wasn't what I'd planned.

Underground, I excavated things:
Myself, a new way of looking,

And looking at it all.
Eventually, a home
And family.
I volunteered again. You could say
I did it right this time.

But no one would.
And if I were caught,
As I was caught,
As I knew I'd be caught,
They'd name only the wrongs,
The mistakes,
The bank,
The violence that made
Her blouse garish.

LEAP TO TRACK. RESCUE MAN. CLAMBER UP. CATCH A TRAIN.
Wednesday, March 18th, 2009

I already told
That other officer, but OK.

All I'm doing is waiting for the C.
I have an audition to get to.
I'm an actor—you know, imagine that.
In a city full of them.

So this guy is standing really
A little too close to the edge
And I don't know, maybe
He has a seizure or
He's been drinking, but anyway,
There's something wrong—
I don't know what. And as he leans
Back against what may seem

Like a cushion of air,
Gravity comes into play
And his overcoat flies up
Almost like it was attached to strings
On the ceiling and

Now he's not there.
He was just there.

I run over and look
And he's there,
Down. He's bleeding.
The dark makes it hard to see him,
And I'm surprised by that, by how
Dark it is. No, but dark is good
Because it means no train for now.
This guy isn't big, but he's unconscious
Which makes you weigh
About twice as much.
I hoist him to the edge
And some other folks grab him
And then they grab me
And as I get pulled upwards back
Into the grimy light,

I see the cleaner light of the train
And now I can get on it, now I
Can go to my audition.

I'm pumped.
It's a good thing I just did
Without really thinking about it.
There is fortune all around me.

NATASHA RICHARDSON, ACTRESS, DIES AT 45
Wednesday, March 18th, 2009

From Roy to Michael to Vanessa
She descends,
The family talent intact
And at her command.
She has been trained, educated, tested.
Her cup runneth over.
She appears to acclaim, but not
Too much—enough to satisfy, but not
Enough to poison.
The cure is in the dose.

When she falls, it's nothing.
Or seems like, but it turns out to have
The throwaway subtlety
Of an onstage gesture;
The kind that foreshadows
A devastation.

She falls, she gets up, she jokes
And laughs and refuses treatment
Because she's young and
She feels fine and
Is maybe a little embarrassed, not

Here, in her real life, wanting
To draw attention.

This last hour
Or two of consciousness is all
Innocence, all unseeing.
She doesn't know that

The fall has nicked open
Something
That should never be unsealed,
And which now
Pours forth, Pandoric,
Like confession, blood
Into a cavity not designed
As a cup.

WHITE HOUSE WILL GET
A VEGETABLE GARDEN
Thursday, March 19th, 2009

Mrs. Roosevelt was the last
To plant vegetables here
On this formal lawn
Which might as well be
At the top of Everest
For all the real air it has.

In this new garden, they will grow
Herbs and lettuces and
Plain things, perhaps.
Carrots and potatoes and
Things the girls will eat willingly.
There may be peas,
Tiny green coins tucked into
A seamed green wallet.

The pastry chef
Looks forward to berries.

Anything so sweet and tender
Can hardly be formal,
Can hardly be artificial,
As it submits to be pressed into dirt
By a thumb, perhaps, or a dowel,

And splits open:
A miniature book
About water, dirt and sunlight.

Offering a first green hint
To the air, it's all a luscious brush
Escaping the earth's ferrule.

TRAVELERS, YOUR TOUR BUS IS BOARDING FOR BASRA
Friday, March 20th, 2009

Maybe it's because we're old
And so it doesn't much matter if we die,
But we're the first
Sanctioned tour of westerners,
Senior citizens all, since the war began.

We have seen Karbala, Najaf, Samarra.
The checkpoints consume
Hours and patience.

The Ministry of Tourism and Antiquities
Has provided security, but we
Don't want it—it feels too restrictive.
We want to see.
We laugh
About how the antiquities are us.

So we take our minibus
Around this neighborhood, lit
Only spottily. We are
Looking for cold beer—
Like teenagers, someone says.

It's hot, and a beer would hit the spot.

We find some, eventually, in a little
Faded corner store with a countertop
Long ago brushed white.

There is no such thing
As a six-pack. The owner
Slides the bottles, one
By one, across the painted countertop.

They're cold and wet.
They leave tracks, a straight,
Faint line of condensation
Connecting us to him.

SON OF SYLVIA PLATH COMMITS SUICIDE
Monday, March 23rd, 2009

While he, at one, slept near his sister
In a bedroom sealed
Against an endless sleep,
His mother looked in the grim oven
For answers.

His father's lover
Searched the same cavity
And found the same black subtraction
Lying on the mattress
Grave with their daughter.
Gone, gone:
Two women and one girl.

Did he
Read everything his parents wrote?
How to find himself on those
Too-examined pages
Smudged by the scholarship of strangers,
Each drawn to the
Extravagant drama?

What's left is
A personal illiteracy.

How to decode
Himself in their texts? It is
Not him, but
His parents' experience
Of him;
The difference
Between him
And the mirror's answer.

He of the mythic parents
And familial depression
Found his answers in what amounted
To an unbroken trek:
Water, fish, migration.

Perhaps movement calmed him.
What whirled in his brain
Was the same as for any of us.

He and his sister
Had what was theirs
Alone.

  This, and what formed
The communal inheritance: the
Beloved stone, especially, with
His last name gouged and blackened.

He struggled,
Unlike the fish.

Light silvered the water.

He fashioned his own
Answer from a rope. It
Loops into any letter.
He chose an O:
A hole through which he could climb.

The rope might have been
Advantageous, benign, connective—
Used to haul something other
Than this man
Into that darkness.

AS CLINTON VISITS MEXICO, STRAINS SHOW IN RELATIONS
Tuesday, March 24th, 2009

Supply-and-demand
Has a deadly cast.
In a little over a year,
7,000 deaths: bodies found everywhere
From garages and offices
To the middle of the street
In the middle of the day.

Street value means something else
When the man lying on the pavement
Stares straight into the sun
With no concern for blindness.
His hands are beyond grasping
Anything, but they hold both noon
And the shadows of his fingers:
Fallen pillars.

You are an editor, a reporter,
A mayor or a policeman.
If you're suspected of talking,
Or even thinking of talking,
One of these businessmen
Might drop by for a visit

With your mother or
Your wife. He might
Bring flowers. He depends
On your mother or
Your wife to tell you. He knows
That you've hidden things—
You've shared only some
Of what frays your
Working hours.

Javier came by. No, nothing—
We just had a drink and talked.
Can you believe these flowers?

You swallow as though you were there
With them, having that drink.
You avoid her gaze, look over
At the dispersing entropy
Of dust floating in the blinds'
Slatted light.

You don't bring any of this up;
You admire the flowers.
You imagine what the next visit
Might involve.

RUSSIAN ROCKET
CARRIES SPACE TOURIST
Thursday, March 26th, 2009

You have sprung from landscape
To aerial night.
Kazakhstan retreats.

The wrong end of a telescope
Swallows down the world
As the rocket turns from gravity,
Its earth-end a fury of burning.

Nine minutes
To orbit. A silver marble in a child's
Hand-held tipping game, the rocket
Slots into position and
Begins to circle, a slim hand
Spanning the clock of the world.

SWEPT UP IN GLOBAL CRISIS, A TOWN'S LONE BANK FAILS
Friday, March 27th, 2009

Lone bank in town, hell,
It's the only bank in Glascock County.
There's only 3,000 souls here, so
Not like we needed more than one.

I called the manager last week.
Told him I found a car,
Needed a loan. He goes,
Go ahead, write the check, I'll
Deal with it Monday when
The check comes in. All right, now,
I got to get back to my hand here.
I'm close to a full house.

That car, now, I don't know what
About my loan. I don't know
Where that stands. Nearest bank
To here, it's about probably fourteen
Miles. Maybe that's who's got the
Paperwork, I don't know.
Waiting on someone to call
About that.

WHOSE FATHER WAS HE?
Sunday, March 29th, 2009

He is found
On the Gettysburg killing fields,
No identification, no badges or stripes,
No pocket diary or letters to place him.
But

He clutches an ambrotype: three
Children, well-dressed and solemn.
Perhaps their mother
Is seated in the room
Behind the photographer.

Perhaps she had sewn
The girl's checked dress
And the older boy's matching jacket.
Perhaps she is telling them
To hold still as

Their father holds still—
A holding beyond his doing.
Like the rest, he looks as though he's
Only resting. His ankles are crossed; he
Gazes up and doesn't
Take in the sky.

These now-untroubled men form
A dire statuary.

Black swarms
Speed them to earth: dust
To dust. There are caps, boots, and
Even hands in the trees: ruinous
Ornaments foretelling a first
Fatherless Christmas.

The witnessing pastures
Are a town-filled vault, open
To the silent blue.

As the armies take their dead
Away, far away
His wife waits,
Waits,
And begins to know.

APOLOGY OFFERED
AT KHMER ROUGE TRIAL
Tuesday, March 31st, 2009

The skulls are stacked

Neatly, like cups, like bricks,
As though they could be built into
Something more useful
Than humans.

We say *flesh and blood*.
But here is
The architecture.

Now in his 60s, he stands up,
A little bent.
He qualifies:
I am being made a scapegoat.
I had to follow orders.
My current plea is that I would like
You to please
Leave an open window for me
To seek forgiveness.

A window offers sunlight,
Air, escape.

The skulls offer
So many corrugated mouths
Open with something
Past speech.

AMID BINGHAMTON GUNFIRE, PLEAS TO POLICE AND HEAVEN
Saturday, April 4th, 2009

The thing that connects them
Is that they don't speak English.
They come
To the American Civic Association
To learn. When class is over,
They laugh and roll their eyes
At the ridiculousness
Even as they practice
What to say when they leave:
Catch you on the flip side and
See you later, Alligator.

Cuban, Russian,
Vietnamese, Polish:
They all need the same tools.

Just before,
They were guessing what
In the black might mean.

They worked on pronouns:
He, we.

Whatever language was their own
Began streaming this bold word
Across their brains as they heard
Shots:
Hide.

In the storage room, they left
The lights off
And tried to make themselves small.

They waited. A Kurdish student
Turned to her teacher, defeated.
She whispered: *They fire in Iraq.*
They fire in the United States.

Holding hands
Means the same thing everywhere, so
They held hands and
Waited for good news
In any tongue.

DEATH TOLL IN ITALIAN
QUAKE RISES TO 150
Monday, April 6th, 2009

L'Aquila is the epicenter. Central Italy,
East of Rome. The nuns
File out of the abbey in their bathrobes.
They look to heaven,
And around.
They are elderly, mostly.
They have seen many wraths:
Mussolini and the Nazis, but this
Is a smashing of God's own fist.
They look up and see that the cupola
Of Santa Maria del Suffragio is
Cracked: a wholeness raggedly halved.
Upheaval's hieroglyphics are
Everywhere they look.
Everywhere, buildings have collapsed.
The nuns look to their own now
Before they turn their attention
To those in need.
They look at the nave's stucco
Ceiling on the floor,
The shattered baptismal font,
The transept fuming with a dust
Made golden in the morning light.

ANSWERING BASEBALL'S WHAT-IFS
Monday, April 6th, 2009

I am almost eleven years old
And lying across my parents' bed.
The radio is on: KDKA.
It's New Year's Day 1973.
I have seen the Pirates play so I know the
Name, and am shocked to hear:
Roberto Clemente has died
In a plane crash.
He was 38 years old and trying
To deliver aid to earthquake survivors
In Nicaragua.
They never find his body.

Or:

He is welcomed to Nicaragua.
He is used to
Adulation from fans; he is used to heat
And humidity from Puerto Rico.
He waves and grins,
Waves and grins.
He helps unload the plane.
The other men

Want to do it themselves,
But it's his mission, so
He'll work, too. He's not too good
To get his hands dirty; hell,
His hands got dirty
In every job he ever had.
He jokes with them:
This is easier than baseball—
Not so much pressure.

Of course
He returns.
His wife and boys
Are asleep. He looks into the bedrooms,
Sees their faces: cameos on pillowcases.

He lies across the bed for
A minute and watches her.
She is submerged in a dream;
Her eyelids pulse a little. He smiles,
Touches her cheek.

A MOMENT OF HEROISM AFTER A BLAST IN BAGHDAD
Tuesday, April 7th, 2009

Here in Kadhimiya, they have seen
Their share
Of things that have to be seen
To be believed,
And even then.
Police stations blown to bits,
Cafes' transfigurations to ruptured
Abbatoirs because they all thought
That silent man actually wanted coffee.

Today what cleaves the air
With sound and blood
Is in the street: a white Peugeot on fire,
Its passengers already dead, except one:
A baby.

One man does a remarkable,
Counterintuitive thing and reaches
Into the fire,
Lifts out the baby, who sits
On a charred lap but
Isn't even crying.
He takes the baby to the police,

Who tell him: *We don't know.*
The mother is dead, so
Take him home. Feed him.

The man is astonished by nothing,
Having lived here
All his life. He takes the baby
Home, where he lives with his mother.
She cries when she sees her son.

She washes the baby,
Changes him into something clean.

They don't know how
He will sleep, how any of them
Will sleep.

ROMEO IS LATE
FOR DINNER
Wednesday, April 8th, 2009

We both recovered,
With tending by her nurse and the friar.
We look back on those days
With laughter and a little fear.

How could we have been
So ready to throw away
Everything
For just one thing?

We have been children
And adults to each other.
She's still beautiful—my impulsive,
Spoiled girl.

Tonight I'm late coming home when
Once again, Tybalt leaps into my head,
Alive there.
When each of us arose that morning,
We had no idea only
One would see night.

I was trying to stop
What was going to happen.

I was trying to tame
The spiky violence that had sprung up
Before us. I intended nothing else.
He grapples with me
Still and I try to pull back
From that slashing arc,

But it all ends the same way.
No matter how many times I think of it,
It ends the same way.

CAPTAIN STILL HELD BY PIRATES
Thursday, April 9th, 2009

It's just bulgur wheat and vegetable oil,
Nothing romantic about it, but the cargo
Isn't what they're after anyway.
They don't care what's carried; it all
Comes down to ransom.
They know that these strangers'
Lives are worth
Something and it's all
A matter of reaching a price.

The sea is a marketplace, a bazaar
Of populations foreign to each other.
What the world condemns,
They see as commerce.

We have what you want. We will
Name your price.

SITE OF '07 MASS SHOOTING REOPENS FOR A PEACE STUDIES CENTER
Friday, April 10th, 2009

After we were denied
Thirty-two voices, we had
The discussion:
How to say what happened.

To remember
Is one paltry thing. We've done that:
The candles, speeches, memorials.
Spring unfolds its rude palette.

We take the event—the madman,
The gun, the lives
Transgressed—and we try
To dovetail sense and history.

This is the best we could do.
We're reaching for something we
Can't quite see; we're hoping
It's there.

A MEXICAN TRADITION RUNS ON PAGEANTRY AND FAITH
Saturday, April 11th, 2009

The committee tells me there are rules
Once you get the part:
No dating, no drinking, no smoking,
No parties. They tell me,
You have to be in shape
To be Jesus.
The beating is real; the cross is real,
And heavy. You have to carry it
Three miles and then get on it. You can't
Make this stuff up. I mean,
Jesus.

It's not just locals.
We get visitors: Bible tourists
Who take so many
Photographs and videos,
It's almost like they think this is news.

The poor guy who plays Judas gets
Fruit thrown at him. Spectators
Actually bring rotten fruit
And pelt him.
This means they have perfectly good

Fruit sitting at home and instead of
Eating it,
They wait until it isn't perfectly good
Anymore. They let it get disgusting and
Then pick it up
Carefully
And bring it out in public so they can
Hurl it at a fellow human being who isn't
Actually Judas,
Or even someone they know.

On Easter, they do this.
I would certainly like to know
How God feels about it.

Judas tells me
He kind of expects the fruit now.
He says he has an extra lock on his door
At home.

There are hundreds in the cast, but
All eyes are on me: the man with
The cross-shaped burdens of the world
On his shoulders.
He is the main character,
After all. You can imagine.

So I'm in training, kind of. I have to
Do a lot of stuff, a lot of
Physical stuff. Basically everything
He did.

Well, not, you know,
Everything.

GAY VOWS, REPEATED FROM STATE TO STATE
Saturday, April 11th, 2009

It will be our slavery:
The thing we look back on and think,
How did we sleep?

There are notches in doors
And cracks in walls
That admit light and air
And prove the Jeffersonian *précis*
Of equality.

As we look around
And see the influences
Laddering up to align right with law,
We will think about the fact
That all any of us want—
As individuals, as members of the mob,
As worlds entire unto ourselves—
Is to be one among the seething crowd.

LAST VOYAGE FOR THE KEEPER OF THE HUBBLE
Monday, April 13th, 2009

From childhood, I was on tiptoe
Wanting to reach out and up.

Now, like Alice in reverse or back again,
I launch from this square, discharged
Out and up into a sky-hitched colliery,
All of it wider, blacker,
More vast than anything you can
Take in. So my partner and
I look closely

At just one thing: a screw, a gyroscope,
A convex lens of such
Sheen and generous proportion
That it captures all ecumenically.

It sees; we discern. In concert,
This singular eye and our minds
Harmonize image and understanding
As much as is possible
When we are talking about haze,
Gas, dark energy, and
Radiance that has
Predeceased us by eons.

When we pass
Through the South Atlantic Anomaly,
We pierce a froth of particles,
And they, us: shards of sun
Spangling and darting inside us.

Imagine:
Literally being filled with light. I try,
But there is no telling it.

We are fragments
Amidst the isolating glories.

We know we have a job to do, earthly
Machinists that we are. We bend
Our focus
To something we can translate.

We crawl over the white surface,
Brilliant against the dark,
And fix what we can.

DERBY FAVORITES CARRY JOCKEYS AND BAGGAGE
Monday, April 13th, 2009

First the cluster, then
The gestural unraveling of the whole,
Each bright silk a child's flag on each
Burnished spine.

On the track, the race
Is a concussive bloom:
The detonating crash of hooves,
The urgent crops
Conducting air to flanks,
The curses, searing breaths, wind
Serrating past ears to a streaming
Whistle as straightaway and curve
And straightaway and
Curve bend and lengthen
Each to each, until the final barrage of
Voices rolls down and unfurls
Over the first
One who—just
For a split-second—
Forms the cruciform tryst
Of surging body
And finish line.

18 YEARS IN THE MAKING
Tuesday, April 14th, 2009

We two met on that white field
In the dark and later,

We were three.
The room we had to make for him—
The cries shocking the night air,

The refusal of food, the entitlement
To all our hours and thoughts. We
 Put down everything to attend him.

There were delicious rewards:
The skin warmth, the toes
Like candies. The way he batted the flats

Of his hands, delighted,
On the vast sea of his bath.
Then we brought home his sister. Now

We are four. The story is
The same with her, and we realize we
Remember nothing from before
They were born.

They were always here.

They are our year-round garden.
There are
Superstitions and wives' tales and things
Doctors tell us to do.
We stagger through.

These two tumble through time
In photographs. What we thought
We'd remember always is a vapor
Without this flat, colorful
Evidence. From day one to now,

We track the updates
Like a flipbook, as they move
(They never stop moving)
From back to knees to feet:

Their own discriminate evolution
As they climb, heels dripping,
Disregarding their fish selves
In the water that throws back
And swallows down
Their departing reflections.

A FEW NOTES
ON THE POEMS

Most of the poems are self-explanatory via the titles. Where I felt some clarification would be helpful, notes appear below.

EDWARDS ADMITS TO AFFAIR
Page 4

Former Democratic presidential hopeful John Edwards admitted that he had had an extramarital affair in 2006 with Rielle Hunter. Hunter had traveled with Edwards while videotaping portions of his campaign.

A BLIND BOXER
Page 9

Ugandan Bashir Ramathan is one of an estimated half million blind Ugandans. Most subsist day to day and have no access to medical care. Ramathan took up boxing as a way to occupy himself and keep in shape.

DR. DOOM
Page 11

In September 2006, while speaking to economists at the International Monetary Fund, Nouriel Roubini predicted the economic crisis which first became readily apparent in late summer 2008. Roubini, a New York University economics professor, was among the first to grasp the scope of the coming storm. His warnings were not generally taken seriously at the time.

WHAT GEORGE ORWELL WROTE
Page 15

Orwell's copious diaries were finally made publicly available, seven decades after he'd written them. The complete text of these volumes can be found at OrwellDiaries.Wordpress.com.

BUT WILL IT WORK?
Page 24

This was one of the first substantive mentions of possible governmental intervention in the growing economic crisis, specifically having to do with the banking industry.

STATUS OF DEBATE
Page 25

It had become clear that American financial institutions were struggling. The first debate between Barack Obama and John McCain was mired in scheduling conflicts as the candidates tried to decide if they should cancel to concentrate on the looming crisis.

SORRY, I CAN'T FIND YOUR NAME
Page 31

Before Mississippi's March 2008 primary, it came to light that a single county election official had purged the eligible-voter rolls of over 8,000 names—including one Republican congressional candidate. The names were restored by the secretary of state's offices before the primary.

LACK OF PREPAREDNESS
Page 40

Terrorist attacks in Mumbai, India on November 26th, 2008 left 173 people dead, many of them tourists and guests at the Taj Mahal Palace & Tower Hotel.

LEAP TO TRACK
Page 52

33-year old actor Chad Lindsey was standing on a subway platform in New York City when he saw a man fall to the tracks. Lindsey rescued the man. Coincidentally, the stage role Lindsey was playing at the time of the rescue required him to lift another actor (playing a character who couldn't walk) several times throughout the course of the play.

DEATH TOLL IN ITALIAN QUAKE
Page 73

The final death toll was close to 300.

CAPTAIN STILL HELD BY PIRATES
Page 80

Richard Phillips, captain of the cargo ship *Maersk Alabama*, had given himself up to pirates off the Horn of Africa after it became clear that they might otherwise harm his crew. He was held by four pirates in a drifting lifeboat for five days before Navy Seal snipers were able to kill three of his four captors (the fourth had surrendered).

SITE OF '07 MASS SHOOTING
Page 81

Two years after a disturbed student killed 32 students and faculty members (and himself), Virginia Tech University reopened the section of the academic building in which most of victims had died. The 4,300-square foot section of Norris Hall will house the Center for Peace Studies and Violence Prevention.

A MEXICAN TRADITION
Page 82

Passion plays are staged in Christian communities throughout the world. This one, in the Mexican town of Iztapalapa, began as a local expression of gratitude and faith at the end of an 1843 cholera epidemic which had decimated the town.

LAST VOYAGE
Page 86

Astronaut John Grunsfeld had been the chief repairman for the Hubble space telescope for 18 years and was making his final voyage.

The typeface used throughout this volume is Perpetua.

Perpetua was designed in 1925 by Briton Eric Gill (1882 – 1940). Gill had formidable artistic skills. In addition to designing typefaces, he worked as a sculptor, printmaker and stonecutter.

The front cover photograph depicts a black feather lying on a red maple leaf and the forest floor. It was taken by the author in Fredericktown, Ohio.

The back cover author photograph was taken by Lillian W. W. V. Klein in Nags Head, North Carolina.

www.ingramcontent.com/pod-product-compliance
Lightning Source LLC
Chambersburg PA
CBHW022306060426
42446CB00007BA/632